Steve
Jobs

Other books in the People in the News series:

Maya Angelou
David Beckham
Beyoncé
Fidel Castro
Kelly Clarkson
Hillary Clinton
Miley Cyrus
Hilary Duff
Zac Efron
Brett Favre
50 Cent
Al Gore
Tony Hawk
Salma Hayek
LeBron James
Jay-Z
Derek Jeter
Dwayne Johnson
Angelina Jolie
Kim Jong-Il
Coretta Scott King

Ashton Kutcher
Tobey Maguire
John McCain
Barack Obama
Danica Patrick
Nancy Pelosi
Queen Latifah
Daniel Radcliffe
Condoleezza Rice
Rihanna
J.K. Rowling
Shakira
Tupac Shakur
Will Smith
Gwen Stefani
Ben Stiller
Hilary Swank
Justin Timberlake
Usher
Oprah Winfrey

Steve Jobs

by Barbara Sheen

LUCENT BOOKS

A part of Gale, Cengage Learning

GALE
CENGAGE Learning™

Detroit • New York • San Francisco • New Haven, Conn • Waterville, Maine • London

59488

LIBRARY OF CONGRESS CATALOGING-IN-PUBLICATION DATA

Sheen, Barbara.
  Steve Jobs / by Barbara Sheen.
     p. cm. -- (People in the news)
  Includes bibliographical references and index.
  ISBN 978-1-4205-0160-5 (hardcover)
  1. Jobs, Steven, 1955---Juvenile literature. 2. Computer engineers--United States--Biography--Juvenile literature. 3. Apple Computer, Inc.--History--Juvenile literature. I. Title.
  QA76.2.J63S554 2009
  621.39092--dc22
  [B]

                                                          2009022098

Lucent Books
27500 Drake Rd
Farmington Hills MI 48331

ISBN-13: 978-1-4205-0160-5
ISBN-10: 1-4205-0160-7

Printed in the United States of America
2 3 4 5 6 7 13 12 11

Contents

Fame and celebrity are alluring. People are drawn to those who walk in fame's spotlight, whether they are known for great accomplishments or for notorious deeds. The lives of the famous pique public interest and attract attention, perhaps because their experiences seem in some ways so different from, yet in other ways so similar to, our own.

Newspapers, magazines, and television regularly capitalize on this fascination with celebrity by running profiles of famous people. For example, television programs such as *Entertainment Tonight* devote all their programming to stories about entertainment and entertainers. Magazines such as *People* fill their pages with stories of the private lives of famous people. Even newspapers, newsmagazines, and television news frequently delve into the lives of well-known personalities. Despite the number of articles and programs, few provide more than a superficial glimpse at their subjects.

Lucent's People in the News series offers young readers a deeper look into the lives of today's newsmakers, the influences that have shaped them, and the impact they have had in their fields of endeavor and on other people's lives. The subjects of the series hail from many disciplines and walks of life. They include authors, musicians, athletes, political leaders, entertainers, entrepreneurs, and others who have made a mark on modern life and who, in many cases, will continue to do so for years to come.

These biographies are more than factual chronicles. Each book emphasizes the contributions, accomplishments, or deeds that have brought fame or notoriety to the individual and shows how that person has influenced modern life. Authors portray their subjects in a realistic, unsentimental light. For example, Bill Gates—the cofounder and chief executive officer of the software giant Microsoft—has been instrumental in making personal computers the most vital tool of the modern age. Few dispute his business savvy, his perseverance, or his technical expertise, yet critics say he is ruthless in his dealings with competitors and driven more by his desire to maintain Microsoft's dominance in the computer industry than by an interest in furthering technology.

In these books, young readers will encounter inspiring stories about real people who achieved success despite enormous obstacles. Oprah Winfrey—the most powerful, most watched, and wealthiest woman on television today—spent the first six years of her life in the care of her grandparents while her unwed mother sought work and a better life elsewhere. Her adolescence was colored by promiscuity, pregnancy at age fourteen, rape, and sexual abuse.

Each author documents and supports his or her work with an array of primary and secondary source quotations taken from diaries, letters, speeches, and interviews. All quotes are footnoted to show readers exactly how and where biographers derive their information and provide guidance for further research. The quotations enliven the text by giving readers eyewitness views of the life and accomplishments of each person covered in the People in the News series.

In addition, each book in the series includes photographs, annotated bibliographies, timelines, and comprehensive indexes. For both the casual reader and the student researcher, the People in the News series offers insight into the lives of today's newsmakers—people who shape the way we live, work, and play in the modern age.

On His Own Terms

S teve Jobs has always had extraordinary dreams, which he has never been afraid of pursuing despite the doubts of others. As the cofounder of Apple Company and CEO of Pixar, he helped start a technological and entertainment revolution. Point and click personal computers, razor thin laptops, networked business computers, touch screen cell phones, portable digital music devices, low priced music downloads, and digitally animated movies might never have come into being or become so popular if not for Jobs's dreams.

Not an Ordinary Person

Although Jobs is not the actual inventor of these items, he is the visionary whose boldness, passion for technology and design, and ability to inspire others made their creation possible.

A man with many sides, Jobs has been described as charming, egotistical, brilliant, opinionated, charismatic, stubborn, persuasive, and critical. He is not easy to understand. Many people find him mysterious. But one thing is clear: Steve Jobs is not an ordinary person. In 1976 at age twenty-one, he cofounded the Apple Computer Company in his parents' garage. Four years later he was worth more than 200 million dollars. By the time

Steve Jobs is a visionary who helped reimagine the computer industry.

he was thirty, he had lost his job at Apple. Down but not out, he started another computer company and bought Pixar, the computer graphics division of a movie studio. Pixar made Jobs a billionaire. But things were not as rosy at Apple. Without Jobs's vision, Apple struggled. On the brink of bankruptcy, the company brought Jobs back in 1997. In a short time, he made Apple more successful than ever.

Jobs's life story is indeed extraordinary. Even as a child he stood out. He was smarter, wilder, and more of a risk taker than his peers. And, his interests were different. His passion was electronics, which set him apart. Throughout most of his youth he did not fit into the various groups that his classmates formed. Unlike many young people who try to change themselves in order to fit in, Steve did not mind being different. In fact, he reveled in it. "Think Different," which became Apple's trademark slogan, aptly describes the company's founder, who has never shied away from doing just that. Terri Anzur, a high school classmate of Jobs, recalls: "Steve was kind of a brain and kind of a hippie . . . but he never fit into either group . . . He was kind of an outsider. In high school everything revolved around what group you were in. If you weren't in a carefully defined group you weren't anybody. He was an individual in a world where individuality was suspect."[1]

Not Likely to Succeed

When Jobs started Apple with his friend Steve Wozniak, many people laughed at them. They said the two men were too young and inexperienced to run a business. The pair had no money, no place to work, and no experience. Although Wozniak was wary, Jobs had a dream. He believed in himself and the company he was starting. So, he ignored his critics, persuaded Wozniak to do the same, and followed his heart. According to authors Jeffrey S. Young and William L. Simon, Jobs was, "Too young and definitely too inexperienced to know what he couldn't achieve, and ruled by the passion of ideas, he had no sense of why something was impossible. This made him willing to try things that wiser people would have said couldn't be done."[2]

A Wild Idea

Jobs's dream of how that business would change the world was even more outrageous. He believed that computers should be tools for everyday people. Before 1975, computers were huge, complicated, expensive devices that were mainly used by government agencies, universities, and large businesses. Few ordinary people could afford a computer or knew how to use one.

Computers before 1975, like this one for IBM, were huge, complicated devices.

Jobs wanted to change that. He believed that if computers were small enough to sit on a desk, easy to use, attractive, and affordable, ordinary people would feel comfortable having the machines in their homes and would use them to do things like writing letters, keeping address lists, balancing checkbooks, playing games, and drawing pictures.

Many industry experts thought Jobs's dream of personal computers was impractical and unmarketable. Jobs proved them wrong. "From nothingness, the personal computer had become the fastest growing industry in American history, a billion dollar triumph spurred by the dream of one college dropout [Jobs] and the engineering virtuosity of another [Wozniak]," explains author David A. Kaplan. "During one decade, Apple alone reached $1 billion in sales . . . Apple was not only a commercial success—the beginnings of the Information Era—but the societal one that Jobs dreamed of just as much."[3]

Not Giving Up

Despite Apple's tremendous success, much of which was due to Jobs, after ten years at Apple a power struggle ensued and he was fired. Having already achieved more than most people ever dream of, Steve could have rested on his accomplishments. In fact, his friends advised him to retire. But Steve remained true to himself. He loved his work. And, he believed he had more to contribute so he invested in two more companies, NeXT computers and Pixar. Most experts predicted he would fail. Once again Jobs proved them wrong. Addressing the 2005 graduating class of Stanford University, Jobs explained: "I'm convinced that the only thing that kept me going was that I loved what I did. You've got to find what you love . . . Your work is going to fill a large part of your life and the only way to be truly satisfied is to do what you believe is great work. And the only way to do great work is to love what you do . . . Don't settle."[4]

Never Settling

Steve Jobs has never settled. He refused to change in order fit in. He remained dedicated to his ideas despite the doubt of others. And, he went forward after being fired from Apple rather than settling for the easy life.

Jobs has always remained true to himself. "Your time is limited," he told the Stanford graduates, "so don't waste it living someone else's life. Don't be trapped by dogma—which is living with the results of other people's thinking. Don't let the noise of other's opinions drown out your own inner voice. And most important have the courage to follow your heart."[5] This is exactly what Steve Jobs has done. In the process, he has changed the world.

Chapter 1

A Difficult Start

On February 24, 1955, an unwed University of California, Berkeley, student gave birth to a baby boy. She decided to put the baby up for adoption. Paul and Clara Jobs, a machinist and a school secretary, adopted the infant and named him Steven Paul Jobs. Three years later the couple adopted Steve's sister, Patty.

The family lived in San Francisco until Steve was five-years-old. Then they moved to Mountain View, California. It is located in what came to be known as the Silicon Valley, the U.S. capital of technology.

A Willful Child

From the beginning, Steve was a handful. Even at a young age he demonstrated the intensity, strength of will, and desire to set the rules that he would later become known for. For example, as a toddler he woke up at 4 A.M. every morning ready to play. Although his parents repeatedly ordered him to go back to bed, he refused. Realizing it was futile to fight the headstrong child, the Jobses bought him a rocking horse and record player stocked with rock and roll records. This kept him entertained, while the rest of the family slept.

On other occasions his willfulness got him into trouble. For instance, although he was frequently warned against it, he could not restrain himself from sticking a bobby pin into an electrical outlet. The resultant trip to the emergency room did not stop him from swallowing ant poison, which he knew was taboo, or from persuading one of his playmates to do the same. His coworkers at Apple said that Steve could convince anyone to do practically anything, no matter how dangerous or outrageous. "The joke going around said that Jobs had a reality distortion field surrounding him," author Robert X. Cringely explains. "He'd say something and the kids in the Macintosh division would find themselves replying, 'Drink poison Kool-Aid? Yeah that makes sense.'"[6]

Important Influences

In an effort to keep Steve out of trouble, his father took the boy under his wing. Paul Jobs was a mechanical whiz. In his spare time, he bought wrecked cars from junkyards. He rebuilt the cars in his garage workshop and resold them at a profit. Steve spent

Steve's father, Paul, let him work on electronics on a workbench in the garage.

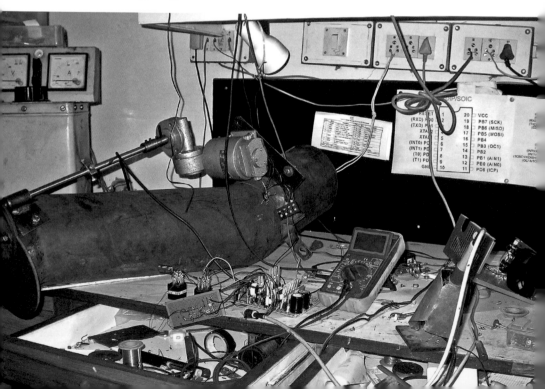

many hours at his dad's side learning about mechanics, electronics, and business. He recalls:

> I was very lucky. My father, Paul, was a pretty remarkable man . . . He was a machinist by trade and worked very hard and was kind of a genius with his hands. He had a workbench out in the garage where, when I was about five or six, he sectioned off a little piece of it and said "Steve this is your workbench now." And he gave me some of his smaller tools and showed me how to use a hammer and saw and how to build things. It was really good for me. He spent a lot of time with me teaching me how to build things, how to take things apart, put things back together. One of the things he touched upon was electronics. He did not have a deep understanding of electronics himself but he'd encountered electronics a lot in automobiles and other things he would fix. He showed me the rudiments of electronics and I got very interested in that.[7]

Many of the Jobs's neighbors were engineers who had garage workshops where they tinkered with electronic projects. One man in particular, Larry Lang, an electrical engineer, took Steve under his wing. Lang had a carbon microphone, which produced sound without an amplifier. The device fascinated Steve. He spent hours questioning Lang about how the device worked. Steve was so single-minded in his interest, that Lang eventually gave Steve the microphone so he could take it apart and study it.

Lang also got Steve interested in building Heathkits. These were kits that provided electronic hobbyists with easy to follow instructions and parts so that they could build their own radios, hi-fi equipment, oscilloscopes, and other electronic devices. Jobs recalls:

> Heathkits were really great . . . These Heathkits would come with these detailed manuals about how to put this thing together and all the parts would be laid out in a certain way and color coded. You'd actually build this thing yourself. I would say that this gave one several things. It gave one an

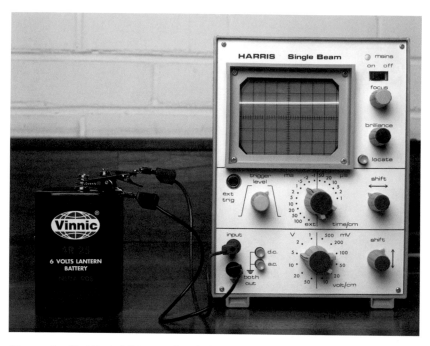

Steve built Heathkits, which helped hobbyists build devices such as this oscilloscope.

understanding of what was inside a finished product and how it worked because it would include a theory of operation, but maybe more importantly, it gave one the sense that one could build the things that one saw around oneself in the universe. These things were not mysteries anymore. I mean you looked at a television set [and] you would think that "I haven't built one of those but I could . . . " It gave a tremendous level of self-confidence, that through exploration and learning one could understand seemingly complex things in one's environment. My childhood was very fortunate in that way.[8]

Pulling Pranks

Spending time with his dad and Larry Lang kept Steve occupied at home. But school bored him. Intellectually, Steve was far ahead

An Influential Teacher

Steve's fourth grade teacher, Imogene "Teddy" Hill, had a lasting influence on his life.

She realized that Steve had a lot of energy that needed to be channeled into learning. But he was rebellious and often refused to do his assignments. To gain his interest, Hill bribed him with candy and money. Once she sparked his interest, she gave him special assignments like building a camera. In an interview with the Smithsonian Institute Jobs talks about the impact Hill had on him:

> I had such respect for her that it sort of re-ignited my desire to learn. . . . I think I probably learned more academically in that one year than I learned in my life. I'm 100% sure that if it hadn't been for Mrs. Hill . . . I would have absolutely ended up in jail. I could see those tendencies in myself to have a certain energy to do something. It could have been directed at doing something interesting that other people thought was a good idea or doing something interesting that maybe other people didn't like so much. When you're young a little bit of course correction goes a long way.

Smithsonian Institution Oral and Video Histories, "Steve Jobs," April 20, 1995. http://americanhistory.si.edu/collections/comphist/sj1.html

of his classmates and did not relate well to them. His mother had taught him to read when he was still a toddler. Indeed, he was already working on electronic projects while his peers were still learning their ABCs. Jeff Eastwood, one of Steve's neighbors and schoolmates explains: "We couldn't understand what he was talking about half the time. He'd show me things that I couldn't understand with all the electronic gear that he'd taken apart."[9]

His intellectual prowess combined with his desire to set his own rules led to trouble. He did not obey his teachers if he did not agree with them. For instance, he often refused to do school work that he had already mastered, saying that he did not see the point. When he did do his work, he usually finished long before the other students. To entertain himself, he concocted complex practical jokes, which he pulled on his classmates and teachers. Such pranks, according to Kaplan, "were a way to show intellectual prowess and rebellion at the same time."[10]

He let snakes loose in the classroom and set off explosives in the teacher's desk. One of his more complicated tricks involved bicycles. He managed to persuade his classmates to give him the combination of their bicycle locks. Then with the help of another intellectually gifted boy, Steve switched the locks on all the bicycles, making it impossible for the other children to unlock their bicycles. "There was this big bike rack where everybody put their bikes, maybe a hundred bikes in this rack, and we traded everybody our lock combination for theirs on an individual basis and then went out one day and put everybody's lock on everybody else's bike and it took them until ten o'clock that night to get all the bikes sorted out,"[11] Steve recalls.

Strength of Will

As a result of all his mischief, Steve was often suspended from school. His teachers thought the best way to keep him out of trouble was to challenge him academically. To determine the best way to do this, Steve was administered an intelligence test at the end of the fourth grade. It indicated that intellectually, he was functioning on a high school level. The school psychologist recommended Steve skip fifth through eighth grade and be sent right to high school.

Steve's parents resisted. Although their son was intellectually advanced, they knew that socially and physically he was still a child. They did, however, agree to allow him to skip the fifth grade. This meant he would start middle school a year early.

His new school was a rough place with many tough, streetwise students. The police were called in often to break up fights. Little learning went on there, and Steve hated the place. To make matters worse, Steve became the target of bullies. He was so miserable at the school that upon completing sixth grade, he threatened to drop out of school if he had to go back there. He was so determined that his parents moved the family to Los Altos, another town in the Silicon Valley, just so Steve could go to a different school. "At eleven years old," authors Jeffrey S. Young and William L. Simon observe, "Steve was already able to demonstrate enough strength of will to convince his parents to resettle. His trademark intensity, the single-mindedness that he could apply to remove any obstacle in his path, was already evident."[12]

The move was good for Steve in many ways. His new school offered advanced classes, so he was intellectually challenged. And, although he did not fit in with any group, he was not harassed there. His parents tried to help him make friends by enrolling

Steve and his friend Bill Hernandez worked with other electronic hobbyists in garage workshops.

him on a swim team. Although Steve was not naturally athletic, he was a good swimmer. Despite his skill, he did not fit in here either. He did not like being part of a team, and he was so intense about winning that he made the other boys uncomfortable. "He was pretty much a crybaby. He'd lose a race and go off and cry. He didn't quite fit in with everyone else. He wasn't one of the guys,"[13] Mark Wozniak, Jobs's former teammate and the brother of his future partner Steve Wozniak, explains.

Fortunately, Steve did not mind being an outsider. He liked being seen as different, and he thought of himself as a rebel. And, he was not completely alone at school. He made friends with another outsider, Bill Fernandez, who shared his passion for electronics. Outside of school, Los Altos contained even more engineers and electronic hobbyists than Mountain View. Bill already knew many of these people and took Steve into their garage workshops. They were happy to share their knowledge and spare electronic parts with the boys. Fernandez explains:

> If you grow up in a woodworking community, with all the tools and professional woodworking around you, and every-one on the block is talking about woodcarving all the time, don't you think the kids will turn out to be good woodwork-ers? We grew up in a town, on streets, . . . and [working in] garages where all we had were the tools for electronics. Isn't it natural that we ended up being pretty good at it, being involved with electronics, doing something in that field?[14]

Meeting Steve Wozniak

In 1968 when Steve was a freshman at Homestead High School, Bill introduced him to an older boy named Steve Wozniak. Woz, as he was known, was a college freshman. He loved electronics and pulling pranks. At the time Woz and Jobs met, the older boy was trying to build a computer-like device from a plan he designed on paper. The device was actually no more than a cir-cuit board to which Woz plugged in connectors and soldered on

The Transistor

The invention of the transistor changed electronics. It, more than anything else, made the personal computer possible.

A transistor is a tiny electronic device that uses silicon to conduct the flow of electricity. Silicon keeps electricity flowing in one direction, which is why transistors are also known as semiconductors.

Before transistors were invented large vacuum tubes were used to conduct the flow of electricity. Early computers, which were gigantic, contained thousands of vacuum tubes. Replacing vacuum tubes with transistors meant that electronic devices, including computers, could be made smaller. Pocket-sized radios were one of the first products to use transistors. Today almost all electronic devices contain transistors. Microchips, which serve as the brains of computers, are basically pieces of silicon embedded with thousands of transistors.

William Shockley, John Bardeen, and Walter Brattain invented the transistor in 1947. The men won the Nobel Prize for their invention in 1956.

microchips. It worked by following a program written on a punch card, which slid into the device. The program made it light up and beep every few minutes.

Fernandez, who was Woz's neighbor, helped him build the device, which eventually blew up. He wanted to show the machine to Jobs, as well as introduce him to Woz. From the start, the two Steves hit it off. Woz recalls:

> I remember—Bill called Steve and had him come over to his house. I remember Steve and I just sat on the sidewalk in front of Bill's house for the longest time just sharing stories—mostly about pranks we'd pulled, and also what kind of electronic designs we'd done. . . . So Steve came into the garage and saw the computer (this was before it

blew up) and listened to our description of it. I could tell he was impressed. I mean, we'd actually built a computer from scratch and proved that it was possible—or going to be possible—for people to have computers in a really small space. Steve and I got close right away, even though he was still in high school.[15]

Nothing Stood in Jobs's Way

It did not take long for the two Steves to become close friends. Working on projects with Woz and Fernandez increased Steve's passion for electronics. He joined the electronics club at Homestead High School, as well as Hewlett Packard's Explorer Club, which offered monthly lectures for young people interested in electronics. It was at one of these lectures where Jobs saw his first real computer. He was fascinated by it and vowed he would own one in the future.

At another Explorer's session, Steve became interested in holographics, a method of producing three-dimensional photographs using laser beams. After the session, he waylaid the lecturer and bombarded him with questions. According to Young and Simon, Steve "had an intensity, driven by whatever his latest passion might be. He would stand very close to whomever he was talking to, invading the person's space as he poured forth about his newest discovery, and he was nearly impossible to avoid once he made up his mind to buttonhole you."[16]

Steve was so passionate about the subject that the scientist agreed to take him on a private tour of the company's holographic laboratory, which was not typically done for private individuals. Then, when Steve got home he called up Bill Hewlett to ask him for spare holographic parts, so that he could build his own holographic device. Hewlett was one of the founders of Hewlett Packard. He was a very important man, and a perfect stranger to Steve. It would not have been surprising if Hewlett had hung up on him. Even then, Jobs was so persuasive that Hewlett not only had a long conversation with the boy, he provided Steve with the

Steve Wozniak was brilliant with electronics and quickly became Jobs's friend.

parts he wanted, and gave him a summer job working for Hewlett Packard. Jobs recalls:

> He was listed in the Palo Alto phone book. He answered the phone and he was real nice. He chatted with me for, like, twenty minutes. He didn't know me at all, but he ended up giving me some parts, and he got me a job that summer working at Hewlett-Packard, on the line assembling frequency counters . . . Well assembling may be too strong. I was putting in screws. It didn't matter. I was in heaven.[17]

A Business Man

Steve could not ask for donated parts for his next project because it involved building an illegal device known as a blue box with Woz. It allowed users to make free long distance telephone calls. To help finance the project, Jobs took a part-time job at a local electronics store. He learned a lot about the value of electronic parts while working there. In fact, he became so knowledgeable that he started buying underpriced parts at flea markets and reselling them to his boss at the electronics store for a profit.

This was Jobs's earliest experience as a businessman, and he liked it. So, once the two Steves had managed to build one blue box, Jobs proposed that they build more and sell them at Berkeley where Woz was attending college. Woz's original intention was to build just one blue box, which the boys would use to pull pranks. In fact, they did have fun with the box. They called the Ritz Hotel in London and made reservations for dozens of nonexistent people. Another time, they called the pope at the Vatican. Although making mischief was enough for Woz, it was not enough for Jobs. He saw a chance to make money and convinced Woz to take part. Kaplan explains:

> Woz . . . liked the intellectual challenge of creating something and of understanding the way things worked. Jobs, by contrast, seemed to see electronics as a means to an end . . .

For Woz, the fun was in the chase; he once told an interviewer that in playing tennis, "the winning isn't as important as the running after the ball." Jobs just wanted to win, and better yet, to sell all the tickets to the stadium. Woz had no ambition. Jobs had nothing but. That desire, combined with his freight-train intensity and golden tongue, made Jobs formidable.[18]

Both Steves contributed to the project in their own way. Jobs got the supplies for the boxes for $40. Woz built the devices. Jobs sold them for anywhere from $150 to $300, depending on how much he thought the customer could afford.

As for their illegal enterprise, it came to an end after Jobs was held up at gunpoint by a prospective buyer. But the pattern that the two young men established of Woz building a product and Jobs marketing it would serve them well in the future.

Chapter 2

Searching for Answers

As a high school student, Steve embraced the counterculture values of individuality, rebelliousness, and experimentation with psychedelic drugs that flourished in the early 1970s. He looked like a hippie. He had long hair, sported love beads, and often went barefoot. At the same time, he was somewhat of a nerd. He was passionate about electronics, developed an interest in poetry and creative writing, and was as intense as ever.

It was at this time that he became involved with Chris-Ann Brennan, a young woman who shared Steve's counterculture values and intellectual pursuits. The two became very close, and they would maintain an off and on relationship for years to come.

In 1972, Steve graduated from high school. He was accepted to many prestigious universities including neighboring Stanford, which was famous for its engineering department and seemed a perfect fit for him. He, however, did not want to go there. "Because," he explained years later, "everyone there knew what they wanted to do with their lives. And I didn't know what I wanted to do with my life at all."[19]

Steve spent the next few years experimenting with different lifestyles in an effort to figure out who he was and what he wanted to do with his life. While Jobs was searching for enlightenment, Steve Wozniak dropped out of Berkeley and started working for Hewlett Packard. The two were at different points in their lives and did not see much of each other.

Reed College

When it came to choosing a college, Steve opted for Reed College in Oregon. His parents did not like this choice. The tuition was more than they could afford. But Steve had made up his mind. He insisted that if he could not go to Reed, he would not go to college at all. His parents were helpless against his strength of will. In the end, they emptied out their savings so that Steve could have his way.

The main reason Steve selected Reed was because it was known for its oddball students and liberal counterculture atmosphere. According to fellow Reed student Elizabeth Holmes, "In the early seventies, Reed was a campus of loners and freaks [eccentrics]."[20]

Even at Reed, Jobs stood out. Robert Friedland, who became Steve's friend, recalls:

> He was always walking around barefoot. He was one of the freaks on the campus. The thing that struck me was his intensity. Whatever he was interested in he would generally carry to an irrational extreme. He wasn't a rapper [talker]. One of his numbers was to stare at the person he was talking to. He would stare into their . . . eyeballs, ask some question and would want a response without the other person averting their eyes.[21]

In addition to Friedland, Steve became friends with Dan Kottke, an intellectually gifted young man who was also trying to find himself. But it was Friedland who had a huge impact on Jobs. Friedland was older than Steve and was somewhat of a celebrity on campus. Steve first noticed Friedland because the older boy dressed in long flowing robes.

Friedland was an outgoing person who could charm almost anyone. He was always the center of attention and was an excellent salesman. He was especially good at captivating a crowd and was handily elected the president of Reed's student council. He soon became Steve's mentor.

Steve was an introvert who had trouble connecting with large

groups. And, because he often felt that he was smarter than almost everyone else, he sometimes came off as arrogant, which did not endear him to others. Steve studied the way Friedland interacted with people and how he captivated large crowds. As a consequence, Steve became more charming and better able to address a large group. This skill served him well when he addressed MacWorld gatherings in the future. According to Kottke,

Robert was very much an outgoing, charismatic guy, a real salesman . . . When I first met Steve he was shy . . . I think Robert taught him a lot about selling, about coming out of his shell, of opening up and taking charge of a situation. Robert was one of those guys who was always the center

Jobs attended Reed College in Oregon.

of attention. He'd walk into a room and you would instantly notice him. Steve was the absolute opposite when he came to Reed. After he spent time with Robert, some of it started to rub off.[22]

Searching for the Meaning of Life

Friedland also inspired Steve in his quest for enlightenment. Indeed, before coming to Reed, Friedland had spent time in jail for possession of LSD. He had experimented with the drug as part of his own quest for enlightenment.

Steve conducted his search for enlightenment with the same intensity as he had conducted his electronic projects. He studied Eastern religions and became a Zen Buddhist, a religion he continues to practice. He tried meditating, experimented with sleep deprivation, and studied the link between diet and physical and spiritual health. He experimented with fasting and different diets, and campaigned for his friends to join him on whatever diet he was currently following. At one point, his diet consisted mainly of carrots. He ate so many that his skin turned orange. He then became a fruitarian and took to showering infrequently. He believed his diet would keep his body clean. "I still believe man is a fruitarian," he told writer Michael Moritz years later. "Of course, back then I got into it in my typically nutso way."[23] Eventually, he became a vegetarian and has followed that diet throughout his life.

While at college, Jobs studied Eastern religions and became a Zen Buddhist.

College Dropout

After one semester at Reed, Steve dropped out. Unlike most college dropouts, he did not leave the campus or stop attending classes. He just stopped paying tuition and dorm fees. With his characteristic rebelliousness, he decided he could have the same experience for free. He slept on the floor of Kottke's dorm room and attended classes in subjects that interested him without getting credit for them. He made friends with the dean of students, Jack Dudman, who was so impressed with the boy that he ignored his illegal actions. Dudman explains: "Steve had a very inquiring

The 1970s

Many of the changes that began in the 1960s, a decade marked by social upheaval, continued to grow in the 1970s. For instance, the hippie culture, which rejected traditional social values and materialism, continued into the early part of the 1970s. Hippies were trying to change society, while experimenting with alternative lifestyles such as communal living, vegetarianism, Eastern religions such as Zen Buddhism, and using psychedelic drugs. The environmental movement also became popular in the 1970s.

The 1970s also witnessed an explosion in technology. The laser, integrated circuit, microprocessor, personal computer, floppy disk, ink-jet printer, pocket calculator, video game, microwave oven, and video cassette recorders were all developed in the 1970s. The fiber optics industry, which transformed communications forever, also had its start in the 1970s.

mind that was enormously attractive. You wouldn't get away with bland statements. He refused to accept automatically perceived truths. He wanted to examine everything himself."[24]

In this manner, Steve was able to satisfy his intellectual curiosity without being forced to sit through required classes that did not interest him. Instead, he attended classes that he might not have experienced had he followed a standard course of study. For instance, he attended a calligraphy class, which influenced his idea that Apple computers have multiple fonts in the future. Jobs recalls:

After six months . . . I had no idea what I wanted to do with my life and no idea how college was going to help me figure it out. And here I was spending all of the money my parents had saved their entire life. So I decided to drop out and trust that it would all work out OK. It was pretty scary at the time, but looking back it was one of the best decisions I ever made. The minute I dropped out I could stop taking the required classes that didn't interest me, and begin dropping in on the ones that looked interesting. It wasn't all romantic. I didn't have a dorm room, so I slept on the floor in friends' rooms, I returned coke bottles for the 5¢ deposits to buy food with, and I would walk the 7 miles across town every Sunday night to get one good meal a week at the Hare Krishna temple. I loved it. And much of what I stumbled into by following my curiosity and intuition turned out to be priceless later on.[25]

A Man with a Goal

In 1973, Robert Friedland went to India. Here, he claimed, he had finally found the meaning of life. Steve decided to go to India,

After dropping out of college Jobs worked for Atari, cor-
recting glitches in games.

too. He wanted Dan Kottke to join him. To earn enough money to make the trip, Steve left Reed and moved back home with his parents. He got a job working for Atari, which at the time was a small company that made video games for arcades. Steve's job was to examine newly designed games and make improvements in them, such as adding sound and correcting glitches. It was the type of work normally done by an engineer. According to Wozniak, the job was "like modifying a program to do different things, just barely a step under designing them yourself and a step that all design engineers go through."[26]

Steve was not highly qualified for the job, but he managed to talk his way into it. Al Alcorn, Atari's cofounder, recalls that Jobs was

> dressed in rags, basically, hippie stuff. An eighteen-year-old drop-out of Reed College. I don't know why I hired him, except that he was determined to have the job and there was some spark. I really saw the spark in that man, some inner energy, an attitude that he was going to get it done. And he had a vision, too. You know the definition of a visionary is "someone with an inner vision not supported by external facts," he had those great ideas without much to back them up. Except that he believed in them.[27]

An Outcast at Atari

The other engineers in the company did not like working with Steve. They complained that he was strange and smelled, which might have been because of his infrequent bathing. But Alcorn insisted on keeping him and arranged it so that Steve worked at night when no one else was present.

Jobs soon reconnected with Woz and often brought his friend into work with him. Woz loved checking out the new games and helped Jobs with his work just for the fun of it. "The best thing about hiring Jobs," Alcorn admits, "is that he brought along Woz to visit a lot."[28]

Atari was the creator of *Pong*, an early two-player video game based on ping pong. The company wanted to develop a similar one-player game. Jobs volunteered to do so for a few thousand dollars.

In reality, he did not have the technical skill to create such a game from scratch, but Woz did. Jobs promised to pay his friend half if he would design the game. Working as a team, the two produced *Breakout* in only four nights. The game was exactly what Atari wanted. Wozniak designed it, while Jobs put all the wires and components of the game together. The two young men worked so feverishly that they both came down with mononucleosis shortly thereafter.

Steve Wozniak

Even as a child, Steve Wozniak was an electronic genius. After high school he attended the University of California at Berkeley where he majored in engineering. But he preferred actually doing engineering projects to studying about them, so he dropped out in the mid 1970s to work for Hewlett Packard. He stayed at Hewlett Packard until he cofounded Apple Computers with Steve Jobs.

In 1981, Wozniak was piloting a small airplane, which crashed. He sustained serious injuries. When he recovered, he decided to leave Apple and go back to Berkeley to get his degree. He used the name Rocky Clark so no one would recognize him. At this time, he also formed a corporation called Unite Us in Song (UNUSON) dedicated to getting computers into the hands of children, and he sponsored two huge rock concerts, which were nonprofit musical and technological extravaganzas.

Wozniak went back to Apple in 1982. In 1985, he and Jobs won the National Technology Medal. He then left Apple for the final time. Since then he has funded many charitable projects, including personally teaching computer skills to school children.

Craftiness Pays Off

Jobs told Woz that Atari paid him $700 for the game, which was a lie. He then paid Woz, half, or $350. It is unclear why he did this. One theory is that since Jobs had set his mind on going to India, he rationalized that he needed the money more than Woz who had a day job with Hewlett Packard. "Steve paid me half the seven hundred bucks he said they paid him for it," Wozniak explains,

> Later I found out he got paid a bit more for it—like a few thousand dollars—than he said at the time. . . . He wasn't honest with me, and I was hurt. But I didn't make a big deal about it or anything . . . I still don't really understand why he would've gotten paid one thing and told me he'd gotten paid another. But you know people are different. And in no way do I regret the experience at Atari with Steve Jobs. He was my best friend and I still feel extremely linked with him . . . Anyway, in the long run of money—Steve and I ended up getting very comfortable money-wise from our work founding Apple just a few years later—it certainly didn't add up to much.[29]

One thing is clear, Jobs did not cheat Wozniak because he was greedy. Indeed, he offered to pay Kottke's way to India because the other boy was poor and could not have afforded the trip otherwise. At the same time, Jobs managed to get Atari to pick up part of his own airfare. The company needed someone to go to Germany to repair some of their video games there. Jobs convinced Alcorn to send him. Jobs successfully did the repairs in less than two hours, and then he proceeded on to India.

India and Back

Jobs and Kottke spent a month in India. When the boys arrived there, they exchanged their western clothes for loincloths, gave away their possessions, and shaved their heads. They traveled the country on foot, begged for food, slept in abandoned buildings

Jobs became disenchanted with India after his visit and returned to work in the United States.

or out in the open, and attended religious festivals. Their goal was to go to the village of Kainchi to meet Neem Karoli Baba, Friedland's guru, who Jobs hoped would help him achieve spiritual enlightenment. When they got to Kainchi, they found out that the guru was dead.

Jobs considered seeking out another guru, but he did not do so. He had not found the answers he was seeking in India. The extreme poverty he saw there caused him to become disenchanted with the country. "It was one of the first times I started thinking that maybe Thomas Edison did a lot more to improve the world than . . . [Friedland's guru] Neem Karoli Baba,"[30] he explains.

He returned to the United States, still searching for answers. He spent time at the All One Farm. It was an Oregon commune, located on land that Robert Friedland owned. Steve ran the apple orchard, which had been neglected until he revitalized it. He also helped the commune to start a successful business selling wood stoves. Despite being happy on the farm, Jobs felt something was missing from his life. He had not found what he was looking for here either, so he moved on.

He took a course at the Oregon Feeling Center, which he hoped would give him answers about who he was and what his role in the world should be. And, he began a search to discover his birth parents, which took years to complete.

Reconnecting with Woz

Still feeling lost, he went back to his job at Atari. He reconnected with Wozniak, who invited him to join the Homebrew Computer Club. It was an electronics club whose members were engineers and electronic hobbyists interested in computers. The club gave them a chance to share their ideas and electronic creations. According to Moritz, "The Homebrew Club provided an audi-

Jobs's outgoing personality helped score free DRAMs for Wozniak.

ence for . . . [individuals] like Wozniak, whose primary interest in life was something that most people couldn't understand . . . In later years the club was fondly remembered as a movable science fair where like-minded souls gathered to share their secrets, display their machines, and distribute schematics."[31] Many of the members were trying to build their own computers, including Woz, who had an idea for a new kind of computer.

Back then computers were gigantic devices. Personal computers or microcomputers as they were known at the time, came unassembled in kit form. They had no monitor or keyboard. Instead they had switches and lights that the user flipped to program. "Every computer up to that time looked like an airplane cockpit . . . with switches and lights you had to manipulate and read," [32] Wozniak explains. He envisioned a completely different kind of computer that worked with a television and a typewriter-like keyboard. Users would type in commands, which would appear on the television screen.

Jobs was enthralled with Woz's vision. Although he was not capable of building such a device himself, he was confident that if anyone could build it, it was Wozniak. Jobs did everything he could to help his friend succeed, including coming up with ideas such as adding a disk for storage, which would be integrated into Apple computers in the future. He also convinced engineers at Intel, an electronics company, to donate rare and expensive computer chips for the project, without which it is unlikely that Woz would have succeeded. "He made some calls and by some marketing miracle he was able to score some free DRAMs [memory chips] from Intel—unbelievable considering their price and rarity at the time. Steve is just that sort of person," Wozniak explains. "I mean, he knew how to talk to a sales representative. I could never have done that; I was too shy. But he got me Intel DRAM chips."[33]

For the first time in a long time, Jobs did not feel lost. He believed that helping Woz to build a computer was more important to the world than his own previous efforts to gain enlightenment. Steve Jobs had found where he belonged and what he was meant to do.

Chapter 3

"We Will Have a Company"

Wozniak finished his computer in 1976. It was a circuit board connected to a television set and a keyboard. When Woz typed in commands, they appeared on the television screen. This was a first in computing.

Woz demonstrated his creation at a Homebrew Club meeting and passed out detailed instructions on how to build it, which the audience grabbed up. But few actually built their own machines. Jobs concluded that the other hobbyists lacked the skill or the time to build them. He reasoned that if he and Wozniak went into business making the printed circuit boards, their peers would buy them. Customers would still have to buy the various components and assemble the machines, but the most complicated part would be done for them. From this small idea, the Apple Computer Company was born.

Wozniak created the computer that launched the company. But it was Jobs's vision and single-mindedness that made the company successful and quirky. Like Jobs, the company was different from anything that came before it.

Apple is Born

When Jobs first suggested that he and Wozniak build and sell the

Jobs and Wozniak agreed to sell circuit boards that Woz created under the name Apple Computers in 1976.

circuit boards, Woz was reluctant to do so. He had no thoughts of starting a business, getting rich, or changing the world. Nor, did he see how such a business could make money. Although he was not materialistic, he did not have money to lose. But Jobs, with his typical intensity, was sure there was a need for such a business. Electronic hobbyists, he insisted, would buy the device. And, if the business failed, at least they could say that they had tried.

Wozniak recalls:

> His idea was for us to make these preprinted circuit boards for $20 and sell them for $40 . . . Frankly, I couldn't see how we would earn our money back. I figured we'd have to invest about $1000 . . . To get the money back, we'd have to sell the board for $40 to fifty people. And I didn't think there were fifty people at Homebrew who'd buy the board. . . . But Steve had a good argument. . . . He said—and I can

Personal Computers

The earliest personal computer was the Altair 8800. Ed Roberts created the first one in his garage in Albuquerque, New Mexico, in 1975. It arrived as a kit that buyers had to assemble. It had no keyboard, monitor, printer, or mouse, and only 250 bytes of memory. That is about the amount of memory a modern computer uses to store one sentence.

The Altair 8800 had switches on a front panel and lights on the back. The user flipped the switches to program the computer. For example, to add two plus two, the user had to flip eight switches for each two, and nine switches for plus. The third light on the left indicated the answer four.

Although Altair 8800 could not do much, hobbyists liked the challenge of entering commands and seeing if their program actually worked. Two teenagers named Bill Gates and Paul Allen developed a programming language called BASIC, which allowed users to load the program on paper tape right into the computer rather than flipping switches. This made computers easier to operate and made it possible for them to do more.

remember him saying this like it was yesterday: "Well, even if we lose our money, we'll have a company. For once in our lives, we'll have a company." . . . That convinced me. And I was excited to think about us like that. To be two best friends starting a company. Wow. I knew right then that I'd do it. How could I not?[34]

Once the two agreed on selling the circuit boards, they had to come up with a name for the company. Jobs, who had recently visited the All One Farm, suggested Apple Computers. He wanted a name that did not sound too technical and would attract everyday people. Wozniak liked the name. On April 1, 1976, Apple Computers was born.

The First Apple Computer

Starting a new company was not easy, especially for two young men whose only business experience was selling illegal blue boxes. They had to come up with enough money to produce the computers, which they named Apple I. So, Jobs sold his van for $1,000, while Wozniak sold his calculator for $250. Jobs also took a job at the local mall, which required him to dress up as characters from *Alice in Wonderland* and shake customers' hands.

The two planned to build fifty printed circuit boards in all. Then Jobs got an order for fifty fully assembled computers from a local electronics store worth $25,000. The store's owner, Paul Terrell, had seen Wozniak demonstrating his invention at a Homebrew Club meeting. He liked what he saw and told Jobs to stay in touch. Jobs's idea of staying in touch was going to Terrell's store the very next morning. Terrell was not enthusiastic about stocking just the circuit boards, but he thought he could sell fully assembled computers. Even though this was not their original plan, Jobs took the order. "That was the biggest single episode in the company's history," explains Wozniak. "Nothing in subsequent years was so great and so unexpected. It was not what we had intended to do."[35]

The Apple 1 computer was sold for $666.66 in 1976.

Producing fifty fully assembled computers meant that Jobs and Wozniak not only had to supply the finished boards but also buy all the components and parts, and put the machines together. With so many computers to make, it was not practical to build the boards by hand. The two decided to have them mass-produced by a manufacturing company. Then, Jobs and Wozniak would plug in the computer chips and do the wiring themselves. However, Woz's graphic representation for the circuit board was hard for the manufacturer to follow. Jobs hired Ron Wayne, an Atari engineer, to draw the schematics based on Wozniak's plans, and also to design an owner's manual. Since they had no money to pay Wayne, they offered him 10 percent of the company.

Wayne did not stay with the company long. He sold back his shares, which become worth $65 million four years later, for $300.

Wayne doubted that Jobs and Wozniak could come up with enough money to pay for all the supplies they needed and the company would fail. Jobs proved Wayne wrong. He convinced a local electronics supply company to give him parts for thirty days on credit. At the same time, he worked out a deal with Terrell to be paid cash upon delivery of the computers. Each machine cost $220 to make. Terrell paid $500 per unit. When Terrell paid Jobs, Jobs used half the cash to pay off the electronic company. In essence, Jobs got Terrell to finance the operation without Terrell knowing he was doing so. Jobs then plowed their profits back into the business.

A Family Affair

Jobs also kept the location of the company's headquarters under wraps. Unable to afford to rent a space, the boys used the Jobs's garage. To make the business seem more professional Jobs got a post office box and an answering service, which kept potential customers from knowing just how modest the business actually was.

The garage was a hub of activity. Wozniak, who was still working at Hewlett Packard, stayed up nights working on the computers, while Jobs spent his days picking up the finished boards from the manufacturer and acquiring supplies. He spent his nights helping Wozniak.

They hired their old friend Bill Fernandez to help them. He was Apple's first employee. Soon, Jobs's sister, Patty, and Dan Kottke were added to the company's payroll. Paul and Clara Jobs helped, too. The group worked round the clock. Patty, Fernandez, and Kottke attached the components to the boards with Jobs's help. They were paid one dollar per board. Wozniak tested each completed board by plugging it into a television set and a keyboard. If there was a problem, he corrected it. From the start, Jobs insisted they use only the best components. While other hobby computers were using static memory chips that used a lot of power, he was adamant that Apple utilize a new chip with dynamic RAM (random access memory or the memory available on a computer). It used up much less power than the old-fashioned chips. Other hobbyists criticized Apple for using the chips, which were more expensive than the static chips. But Jobs was right about their value. Apple I was the first personal computer to use the chips, which eventually became the industry standard. "Steve was pushing to use the right parts," Wozniak explains. "We were lucky to be on the right track. It was one of the luckiest technology steps on the whole development."[36]

In addition to his other duties, Jobs went to dozens of electronics stores trying to sell Apple I. With his typical determination, he often would not leave until the manager agreed to stock at least one machine. In this manner, he managed to sell 150 additional computers, which he and Woz priced at $666.66. They had no idea of the number's Satanic connection (Satan is sometimes represented by the number 666), picking it because they liked the repeating digits.

Improving Apple I

Apple I was very different from modern computers. It was more a computer kit than a complete computer. It had no keyboard, case, or television monitor. Buyers had to supply these

Double Sided,
Double Density,
Soft-sectored
with Hub Ring.

MD-2D
CC-8725-300

Jobs wanted the Apple II to have top of the line technology, including a floppy disk instead of a cassette.

features. It stored data on a cassette tape, and it produced only black and white text and graphics.

Even before Wozniak finished designing the machine, he started thinking of ways to improve it. He wanted his next computer, which he and Jobs named Apple II, to support color, sound, and high-resolution graphics. He also wanted the machine to have slots in the back, which would allow the memory to be expanded. Jobs had ideas, too. He wanted to replace the cassette tape with a floppy disk, a new invention that he had heard about. He was so adamant that Apple II should keep up with new trends that he got a sample floppy disk for Woz to study and re-create. "Steve was always looking for new technologies that had an advantage and were likely to be the trend,"[37] Wozniak explains.

But more than that, he envisioned a future in which computers would become as common and as useful as telephones. Every person would have at least one. At the time, this was considered a wild idea. But Jobs firmly believed in his vision, and he had a plan to achieve it.

He was convinced that if Apple could build fully assembled, easy to use computers the company would change the world. Jobs explains:

> The Apple I took us over a big hurdle, but a lot of people who wanted to use the product were unable to. We were getting some feedback from a fairly small sample—maybe 40, 50 people. We were hearing from dealers too. They'd say, "I think I can sell 10 times more of these if you would just put a case and keyboard around it." That's what a lot of the direction for Apple II came from. If there hadn't been an Apple I, there would not have been an Apple II. The first product solved some of the problems and exposed the remaining ones in a much clearer light. But we were going on common sense. . . . We were thinking we should build a computer you could just roll out of the box.[38]

Presentation, Design, and Marketing

Jobs and Wozniak showed Apple I and a mock-up for Apple II at the Personal Computer Festival in Atlantic City, New Jersey, in the summer of 1976. It was the machine's first national exposure. Their display, which was perched on a wobbly old card table in a dark corner, garnered little attention. The experience made a big impression on Jobs. He realized that if they were going to sell their computers to everyone, not just hobbyists, presentation, design, and marketing were important. With this in mind, he insisted that Apple II be self-contained, meaning it would come with a monitor, case, and keyboard, and that it be small, lightweight, quiet, and attractive. He wanted it to look like a household appliance that the average person would feel comfortable using. To this

end, he insisted that the computer should be housed in a molded plastic case, which, at the time, was more expensive than metal or wood. But, he believed it would make the machine look sleek and modern. Then, he hired industrial designer Jerry Manock to redesign Apple II to fit his vision. He also prodded Woz to give the computer a lightweight power supply that did not need cooling. This would eliminate the need for a fan, making the machine quieter. Finally, he hired an advertising firm to come up with the colorful Apple logo, which has become so recognizable. Then, he kept the firm on to launch an advertising campaign for Apple, which included an ad in *Playboy Magazine*.

Doing all this required more money than Apple had. Jobs went to banks, Atari, and Hewlett Packard looking for an investor. His youth, long hair, and hippie attire did not instill confidence in the business people he propositioned, and he was repeatedly turned down. Finally, he met Mike Markkula. Markkula was a thirty-four-year-old retiree, who had made millions of dollars working as a marketing executive for Intel, the computer chip manufacturer. An individualist himself, he was able to look beyond Jobs's appearance. When Jobs told him about Apple II and his vision for the future, Markkula was hooked. He provided Apple with $92,000, in exchange for a third of the company. As part of his role at Apple, Markkula developed a business plan, which was vital to getting the company off the ground. From the start, he said he would stay with Apple for only four years, and then he would go back into retirement.

The West Coast Computer Faire

In order to get Apple II finished in time for the April 1977 West Coast Computer Faire, Apple added more employees, many of whom worked round the clock. The machine was worth the effort. It was the first easy to use computer ever made. It had color, high-resolution graphics, sound, and a place to attach game paddles. It was also the first computer to have a programming language built into it. For years to come, other computer manufacturers copied it.

The Apple II was a hit for Jobs, left, and Wozniak at the 1977 West Coast Computer Faire.

The computer was the hit of the fair. While most of the other displays looked like those of hobbyists, due to Jobs's resolve, Apple's display was slick and professional. The display, the advertising and marketing that Jobs insisted on, and the innovativeness of Apple II, all put the company on the road to success.

In no time, the company received three hundred orders for the machine. That was just the beginning. By 1978, Apple was turning a $2 million profit. By 1980, it was making $335 million, had more than one thousand employees, and was housed in a huge campus in Cupertino, California. When the company went public, which means that shares of the company were sold on the stock exchange, even more money rolled in. Jobs was suddenly worth more than $217 million, making him the youngest person in history to make the Fortune 400 list of tycoons.

Much of the Apple's success was due to Jobs. Moritz explains:

> It [Apple II] was a product of collaboration and blended contributions . . . The color, the slots, the way in which the

memory could be expanded . . . the control of the keyboard . . . was Wozniak's contribution. Holt [an Apple employee] had contributed the extremely significant power supply and Jerry Manock the case . . . But behind them all Jobs was poking, prodding, and pushing and it was he, with his seemingly inexhaustible supply of energy, who became the chief arbitrator and rejector.[39]

Attention to Detail

One reason for Apple II's success was that Jobs was as concerned about the machine's construction as its appearance. For instance, he insisted that the wires connecting the computer chips on the computer's internal circuit board be perfectly straight, even though nobody saw them. Attention to detail, he believed, showed consumers the company cared, creating a loyal customer base. Throughout his career, Jobs demanded this same attention to detail in all the company's products. Once again, Jobs was right. Apple's customers are extremely loyal.

To make the outstanding products, Jobs hired the most talented people he could find. He treated them more like artists than scientists, trying to inspire them to do their finest work. But he was brash and outspoken and was not considerate of their feelings. Although he made a point of publicly praising Apple employees and rewarding them lavishly with things like cash and stock options, all expense paid vacations, bonuses, and individual research budgets, he also openly criticized and humiliated them if they did careless work. Some found him impossible to work with, while others adored him. "My job is not to be easy on people," he explained. "My job is to make them better."[40]

A Different Company

Jobs also tried to make the company completely different from other workplaces. He did whatever it took to foster creativity. Each building had its own theme and name chosen by the employees.

Apple has different workspaces than most companies to help foster creativity.

For instance one building was named the Land of Oz; it housed the Dorothy and Toto conference rooms. And, each floor had a lounge area equipped with red-topped popcorn stands where employees could visit and share ideas.

In addition, there were no set work hours. Employees came and went at will. When they were involved with a project, many, including Jobs, worked day and night. Nor was there a dress code. Jeans and tee shirts were the norm. Jobs wore a black turtle-neck and jeans almost everyday, an outfit he made famous.

A Confusing Personal Life

Those early days at Apple were some of the happiest in Jobs's career. But things were not going as well in his personal life. Jobs was sharing a house with Chris-Ann Brennan, but he was more interested in Apple than in their relationship. On May 17, 1978, Brennan gave birth to a baby girl, whom she named Lisa. Brennan

Kids Can't Wait

In 1979, few schools had computers. Jobs strongly believed that if every school had at least one computer, it would change students' lives. He proposed that Apple donate a computer to every school in the United States. This would have cost Apple 100 million dollars, which the company could not afford. But, if Apple could donate the computers and take a tax deduction, as was allowed for donations to universities, the cost would be 10 million dollars, which Apple could afford.

Jobs enlisted the aid of California congressman Pete Stark. He and Jobs drafted the "Kids Can't Wait Bill," which made donations of equipment to K-12 schools tax deductible. Jobs spent two weeks in Washington lobbying for the bill.

Unfortunately, the bill never reached the Senate floor. However, the state of California thought the bill was a good idea and passed a similar bill that covered the state. As a result, Apple donated one computer to every school in California. It donated software and provided free training for teachers. Jobs says that getting computers into the hands of children in this way is one of his greatest accomplishments.

said Jobs was the father. For the next two years, he denied the baby was his and refused to pay child support.

In 1980, Brennan took Jobs to court. He was forced to pay child support, but he still refused to see his daughter. No one knows why Jobs acted this way. Eventually, he came to acknowledge and love Lisa, but it took time. In the interim he continued focusing all his attention on his other baby, Apple.

Chapter 4

Down but Not Out

Jobs continued to take Apple to new heights. But in 1985 a power struggle within the company caused Steve to lose his job. He took on new projects, spending almost all his money trying to make them successful. When it looked like he was about to lose everything, he managed to turn things around. Not only did his new projects turn out to be extremely successful, Apple asked him to come back. The company was lost without him. Steve Jobs was Apple.

A New Idea

With his private life in turmoil, Jobs moved out of the house he shared with Chris-Ann Brennan and bought an old mansion in Los Gatos, California. Except for a few cushions and a mattress on the floor of his bedroom, he never furnished it. Nor, did he spend much time in the house. His real home was Apple, where his latest goal was to create a new computer. To help with financing, he got the office machine company Xerox to invest one million dollars in Apple.

A visit to Xerox PARC, the company's research center, provided Jobs with inspiration. He saw a demonstration of a revolutionary computer named Alto that Xerox was working on. It had a point and click graphic user interface.

After visiting Xerox PARC, Jobs saw that a point and click graphic user interface could revolutionize computers.

Until then, it was necessary to type in complicated commands to direct the computer. The point and click graphic user interface allowed users to make selections by moving a pointer to onscreen items, which would open individual windows for different documents and cause onscreen menus to pop up. Although this is standard operating procedure today, back then it was revolutionary. Xerox, however, did not recognize the computer's potential and did not intend to market it. Jobs, on the other hand, immediately grasped the importance of the technology. He recalls, "When I went to XEROX PARC in 1979, I saw a rudimentary graphical user interface. It wasn't complete. It wasn't quite right. But within 10 minutes, it was obvious that every computer in the world would work this way someday." [41]

Macintosh: Revolution in a Box

Jobs went back to Apple obsessed with creating a computer based on the technology he had seen at Xerox. His first try was a computer called Lisa, which was the first computer he worked on without Wozniak's help. He was not happy with the team working on Lisa, or with the computer, which was large and expensive.

A Private Individual

Although Steve Jobs loves talking about his various businesses, he is less forthcoming about his personal life. Little is known about how Jobs spends his wealth. He is not very materialistic. He dresses in jeans, tennis shoes, and black turtleneck shirts. He lives with his family in an average size ranch-style home in a middle-class neighborhood in Palo Alto, California, near Stanford University.

Although he is involved in charitable pursuits, he rarely speaks of them. It is known that he set up charities in India that help poor blind people.

Otherwise, he admits to being happily married, a Zen Buddhist, and a vegetarian. In fact, he bought a vacant house next door to his own house and tore it down in order to turn the lot into a large organic garden. Here, he grows many of the foods his vegetarian family consumes. He is so enthusiastic about vegetarianism and eating healthy that he insisted the vending machines at Apple and NeXT offered healthy snacks. On Halloween, he hands out little bottles of carrot juice to trick or treaters.

It was not the type of computer that the average person would buy. So, in 1981, even before Lisa hit the market, Jobs turned his attention to another new computer, the Macintosh (Mac), a low-priced, user-friendly machine, conceived of by Apple engineer Jef Raskin. It meshed perfectly with Jobs's vision of the future. The Macintosh was a computer for the average person. It would, Jobs insisted, change the world.

Although Raskin came up with the original idea for the Macintosh, it was Jobs who brought the machine into existence. He handpicked an extremely talented team of about forty scientists to build it, housed them in a separate building that flew a pirate flag, and told them that it was better to be a pirate than to join the navy. By this, he implied that it was okay to break the rules.

Pushing the Mac Team

The Mac team was Apple's elite and Jobs let everyone in the company know it. He gave team members medals, took them to restaurants, served them freshly squeezed orange juice each morning, surprised them with cash bonuses, and provided them with first-class plane tickets. He even put a video arcade and a piano in the lobby, so they would feel at home.

At the same time, Jobs was a strict taskmaster. He routinely stood over team members' shoulders, asking questions and fiddling with their work. When he did not like what he saw, he yelled and criticized until changes were made. He fired team members whose work did not live up to his standards. If he was harsh, it was because he believed that the Macintosh was going to change computing. He envisioned it as a revolution in a box.

Jobs insisted that the Mac be the most technologically advanced computer of its time. He was adamant that it be half the size of other computers and extremely easy to operate. It also had to have a graphic user interface, multiple fonts, support sound, drawing, and painting, and a have a mouse, which was a brand-new invention that he had heard about. Such a machine had never been built before.

Jobs rewarded the Mac team but also strictly scrutinized every step of their work.

But Jobs's team was the best around and he expected the impossible from them. And, he convinced his team that they were capable of building it. More than that he made them believe that they were about to change the world. According to Mac team member Trip Hawkins,

> Steve has a power of vision that is almost frightening. When he believes in something, the power of that vision can literally sweep aside any objections, problems, whatever. They just cease to exist. The reason that Apple succeeded is that we really believed in what we are doing. The key thing was that we weren't in it for the money. We were out to change the world. [42]

The Macintosh was a revolutionary machine. It was, according to technology writer Leander Kahney,

> Designed for ordinary people, not programmers, it dispensed with blinking cursors and inscrutable instructions for a child-friendly interface navigated by a simple . . . pointing system, the mouse . . . It played music, drew pictures, and could speak for itself in a synthesized voice. As it booted up, a friendly, smiley face shone from the screen. . . . The technology was a good 10 years before its time. [43]

And, just as Jobs envisioned, it brought ordinary people to computing.

Jobs is Out

The Macintosh entered the market in 1984. Jobs spent over $1 million dollars advertising it, including a Superbowl XVIII commercial. At first, sales were remarkable, but then they slowed. Jobs predicted Apple would sell two million machines in the first two years, but he was overly optimistic.

Industry wide, computer sales were poor and Apple was feeling the slump.

The company was now a huge $2 billion corporation with

When Apple sales slumped, John Sculley, center, lost faith in Jobs's vision.

over seven thousand employees. Markkula and Wozniak were gone. A year earlier, Jobs hired John Sculley, the former CEO of Pepsi, to preside over Apple. At first the two men got along well, with Sculley accepting Jobs's vision of computers as household appliances. But when Macintosh sales dipped, Sculley lost faith in Jobs's vision. "Apple was supposed to become a wonderful consumer products company," Sculley said. "This was a lunatic plan. High tech could not be designed and sold as a consumer product." [44]

Sculley was wrong, but nobody knew it at the time. He felt the only way to boost Macintosh's sales was to make the machine more like a computer designed for business use. In order to do this, he wanted to reorganize Apple and put someone other than Jobs in charge of the Macintosh division, which had swelled to over seven hundred people.

Jobs rebelled against this plan. He tried to get the company's board of directors to fire Sculley and make him the CEO. But this did not happen. The board voted against Jobs.

Jobs lost control of the Macintosh division. Although he was given the title of chairman of Product Development, he was stripped of any real power. In 1985, his office was moved off the main Apple campus to a building where he rarely came in contact with other Apple employees. He recalls:

> I was asked to move out of my office. They leased a little building across the street from most of the other Apple buildings. I nicknamed it Siberia. So I moved across the street, and I made sure that all of the executive staff had my home phone number . . . I wanted to be useful in any way I could . . . but none of them ever called. So I used to go to work. I'd get there, and I would have one or two phone calls to perform, a little bit of mail to look at. But most of the corporate management reports stopped flowing by my desk. A few people might see my car in the parking lot and come over and commiserate. And I would get depressed and go home in two or three or four hours, really depressed. I did that a few times, and I decided that it was mentally unhealthy. So I just stopped going in.[45]

NeXT Computers

Jobs spent his newfound spare time at the Stanford University Library. Here, he met Paul Berg, a biochemist studying gene therapy. When Jobs learned that it often took Berg two weeks to run a single test, he got the idea of building a computer in which students and researchers could simulate experiments. From this idea, NeXT computers was born. The company, he proclaimed, would make: "A radically new machine that might enable some obscure kid to simulate a multimillion dollar microbiology laboratory on his screen and then find a cure for cancer."[46]

In September 1985, Jobs officially left Apple, taking five members of his Macintosh team with him. He sold all but one share of his stock in the company to fund NeXT. He immediately hired the most gifted engineers he could find. Like his Macintosh team, these engineers, too, believed that their work would change the world.

Of course, Jobs demanded that everything at NeXT precisely fit his vision. The building that housed the company had to be an architectural masterpiece. The factory had to be kept spotless. And the computer itself had to have revolutionary technology and impeccable style.

This demand for perfection cost Jobs $10 million in the first

After leaving Apple in 1985, Jobs launched NeXT computers.

Tech Talk

The world of computers has a language all its own. Here are a few computer terms and their meaning:

application: A software program that runs on a computer.

BASIC: A popular computer programming language used in the creation of software.

bit: The smallest unit of data in a computer.

byte: A unit of data equal to eight bits. Bytes are used to measure file size and computer memory.

CD-ROM: A compact disk that can be read by a computer.

Central Processing Unit (CPU): The chip that instructs the computer on how to run. It is basically the brain of the computer.

chip or microchip: A tiny electronic device whose circuitry acts as memory for the computer.

data: Information stored or processed on a computer.

hardware: The actual computer and the components that comprise it.

motherboard: The circuit board within a computer.

network: To connect two or more computers with each other so that they can communicate with each other.

Random Access Memory (RAM): The memory available to computer programs. For instance, a computer with 10 MB RAM has 10 million bytes of memory.

software: Programs that can be run on a computer.

three years. It also slowed down the completion of the computer, which was not released until 1988. It was a sleek black cube with groundbreaking multimedia capabilities such as full motion video, animation, and the ability to record and store voice messages. However, these innovations came at a steep price. The computer cost $6,500, much more than the average college professor or student could afford. And, although universities were impressed with the machine, most universities received donated business computers for free, so they were reluctant to purchase Jobs's creation. The computer did not sell and the company that Jobs thought would be his greatest triumph was losing money.

Pixar

At the same time that Jobs was starting up NeXT, he got involved in another business venture. In 1986, he bought controlling shares in the computer graphics division of *Star Wars* producer George Lucas's film company for $10 million. At the time, the company, which Jobs renamed Pixar, was developing computer-generated imagery, which they hoped would replace traditional special effects and hand-drawn animated movies. They had already created a computer and special software for this purpose. The computer was extremely technical and expensive, costing $135,000. When Jobs saw their work, he was awestruck.

Jobs got the idea of producing and selling the Pixar computer. He imagined doctors using it to enhance MRI and X-ray results, or to create three-dimensional images of a patient's body. Although such technology is now common, at the time hospitals were reluctant to spend $135,000 for the machine, and the computer failed to sell.

At the same time, Pixar's animation division was losing money at a rapid pace, and it all was coming out of Jobs's pocket. Jobs considered shutting down the animation division of the company. But he believed that given time to develop, computer animation would change motion pictures. He did not interfere with the company's creative division because he knew very little about computer animation. Instead, he wrote check after check to keep

Jobs believed that Pixar's animation division would change motion pictures and be successful.

it open. In a few years, he had spent $50 million. In 1988, he funded the production of *Tin Toy*, one of the company's earliest computer animated films. According to Young and Simon, "It was a pivotal moment in Pixar's history."[47] *Tin Toy* would go on to win an Oscar for the best animated short film and would be the inspiration for Pixar's first full-length movie, *Toy Story*. But those successes were still in the future.

Ups and Downs at Home

Steve's personal life was also having its ups and downs. In 1986, his mother Clara Jobs died of cancer. His father had died years earlier. His mother's death hit Steve hard. He found that working helped him deal with his grief.

At the same time, new people were entering his life. He had accepted his daughter Lisa into his life and was on amiable terms with Chris-Ann. His long term search for his birth parents led him to Joanne Simpson, his birth mother, and his sister Mona Simpson, with whom he became quite close.

In 1989, he met Laurene Powell at a lecture he gave at Stanford University, where she was a graduate student studying business administration. Jobs was immediately struck by Powell's beauty and made a point of speaking to her. He found that she was as intelligent as she was attractive, and she was a vegetarian, like Jobs. The two hit it off immediately. "We walked into town," Jobs explains describing their first date. "And we've been together ever since."[48]

The couple was married in a Buddhist ceremony in Yosemite National Park on March 18, 1991. The wedding was like Jobs, unconventional and informal. The couple's first child, Reed, a son named after Reed College, was born in September 1991. Two daughters followed, Erin in 1995 and Eve in 1998. Jobs had finally become a traditional family man, and he loved it. He could often be seen in-line skating with Lisa, playing ball with Reed, or pushing a baby carriage around the home in Palo Alto where the Jobs family lived.

Success from Failure

Unfortunately, Jobs's businesses were not going as well as his personal life. Pixar and NeXT were losing a combined $60 million a year. In order to turn things around, Jobs made dramatic changes in both companies. He closed the hardware and sales division of NeXT, turning the business into a software company intent on developing a computer operating system able to compete with Microsoft's newly released Windows, which it did.

The Disney/Pixar collaboration Toy Story was a huge hit and made Jobs a billionaire overnight.

At the same time, he sold the computer division of Pixar, but left the creative computer animation division intact. He believed that someday it would change the motion picture industry. "Pixar's vision was to tell stories—to make real films," he explains. "Our vision was to make the world's first animated feature film— completely computer synthetic, sets, characters, everything."[49]

Until that happened, Pixar was costing Jobs a fortune. After *Tin Toy* won an Academy Award, he got help. In 1991, Jobs managed to convince the Disney corporation to fund, promote, and distribute three full-length Pixar movies, a miraculous feat of persuasion since Pixar was losing so much money.

Four years later Pixar came out with *Toy Story*. It was a smash hit. As Jobs imagined, its success launched the computer-animation film industry.

Taking advantage of the movie's popularity, Jobs took the company's stock public. It was a bold action because the company was not yet turning a profit. But the public believed in Jobs. The initial price for the stock was $22 per share, but the demand was so great that it rose to $39 per share in just one day. Jobs, who owned thirty million shares, became a billionaire overnight.

Return to Apple

In the decade since Jobs's departure, Apple also had its ups and downs. By 1996, the company was losing money. It had also lost its reputation as an unconventional, cutting-edge company. Apple computers no longer boasted an innovative design, or the same attention to detail they had been known for.

Sculley had been forced out in 1993. The new CEO, Gil Amelio, thought that Apple computers needed a new innovative operating system. He wanted Apple to buy NeXT to get their operating system. He also wanted to rehire Jobs. He thought bringing Jobs back would excite the public and raise Apple's sales. "I'm not just buying software. I'm buying Steve Jobs,"[50] Amelio said at the time.

Although he rarely talked about it, Jobs still missed Apple. A few months earlier, when Karen Steel, a former Apple employee who followed Jobs to NeXT, returned to Apple, Jobs wistfully told her: "It must feel like you're going home."[51]

Jobs secretly longed to go back to the company he had started in his garage. He was even more eager to unload NeXT, but he was too shrewd to let Amelio know how he felt. Driving a hard deal, Jobs got Apple to pay him $377.5 million dollars for NeXT plus 1.5 million shares of Apple stock, a very high price for a losing company. As part of the deal, Jobs agreed to return to Apple as an informal advisor. It was December 1996. Much to his joy, Steve Jobs was going home.

Chapter 5

Into the Future

When Steve returned to Apple, the company was in shambles. Jobs's innovative ideas not only saved the company but took Apple to new heights. Today it is one of the most successful corporations in the world, which is largely due to Jobs.

Befriending a Rival

Apple lost $1.6 billion under Gil Amelio. When Jobs saw the mess the company was in he started campaigning for change. In July 1997, the board of directors fired Amelio and offered Jobs the CEO slot. He turned down the offer but agreed to serve as interim (temporary) CEO. He also turned down the board's offer of a huge salary, opting for one dollar a year instead. This was not unusual for Jobs. He had not taken a salary at NeXT, and his top salary at Pixar was $50. Jobs had more money than he needed. He was more interested in getting Apple back on track than in getting richer. Jobs explains: "I was worth about over a million dollars when I was twenty-three and over ten million dollars when I was twenty-four, and over a hundred million dollars when I was twenty-five and it wasn't that important because I never did it for the money."[52]

Apple lost over $1 billion under Gil Amelio, right, and Jobs returned to Apple as interim CEO.

Jobs knew he had to take some radical steps to save Apple. One of the first things he did was make a deal with Microsoft. In exchange for $150 million, all Macintosh computers would use Microsoft's Explorer web browser and its Office software. Jobs announced the deal in August 1997 in front of a large audience of Apple devotees at the annual MacWorld Conference and Expo in Boston. This audience booed the announcement.

In the past, Jobs had accused Microsoft of stealing the idea for Windows from Macintosh. Many Apple devotees looked at Microsoft as the enemy, and they felt betrayed by Jobs. But Jobs knew that this was the best way to help Apple financially, and he was right. The value of the company's stock rose 33 percent as a result of his action.

He is Back

With enough money to keep the company afloat, Jobs turned his attention to Apple's employees and products. He seemed to be everywhere. He spent hours walking around the Apple campus, questioning whomever he met about who they were and what they did. He also held meetings with different groups of employees where he grilled them about the products they were working on. It was up to each employee to convince Jobs that their product had value. On a few occasions, his blunt manner and probing questions reduced employees to tears.

Through these exchanges, Steve identified those people with innovative ideas, and those he considered dead weight, firing the latter. "Steve tests you, challenges you, frightens you," explains Todd Rulon-Miller who worked for Apple. "He uses this tactic to get to the truth . . . It's his way of asking: 'Do you believe in what you're saying?' If you wither or blather, you're lost."[53]

Once Jobs was satisfied with Apple's staff, he worked directly with the hundreds of employees who were not fired. Nothing was done without his knowledge. Not even a paper clip was purchased without his okay. Jobs had taken over.

Think Different

The next change he made involved advertising. Apple had lost its image as a hip, renegade, cutting-edge company. That image, which was in many ways a reflection of Jobs, helped distinguish Apple from other more traditional computer companies. Many Apple customers thought of themselves as rebels. When the company's outsider image faded, so did this customer base.

Jobs hired an advertising company to resurrect Apple's image. With Jobs's input the company came up with the slogan "Think Different," which was scrawled atop pictures of innovative thinkers like Albert Einstein, John Lennon, and Mahatma Gandhi, to name a few. It was created not only to improve Apple's sales, but also to remind Apple employees what the company had been, and what it could be again. "When I got back here, Apple had forgotten who we were," Jobs explains.

> Remember that "Think Different," ad campaign we ran? It was certainly for customers to some degree, but it was even more for Apple itself. You can tell a lot about a person by who his or her heroes are. That ad was to remind us of who

Jobs's innovative marketing campaign featured John Lennon and Yoko Ono next to Apple's "Think Different" slogan.

our heroes are and who we are. We forgot that for a while. Companies sometimes forget who they are. Sometimes they remember again, and sometimes they don't.[54]

The iMac

Jobs's changes were working. Five months after he took over the company, it was turning a profit. With Apple heading in the right direction, he turned his attention to the iMac, short for the Internet Macintosh. It was a new computer, which Steve envisioned as an inexpensive, easy to set up and use machine that allowed users to easily access the Internet.

Keeping with the "Think Different" slogan, Jobs wanted the iMac to look different from other computers. The computer, monitor, and speakers were all contained in a clear oval shaped case with fruit colored trim. It also had a keyboard that lit up when it was touched. The machine, which debuted in 1998, was an immediate success. By the close of the year more than 800,000 were sold. Many of the buyers were first time computer owners who were taken by the machine's stylish design and the ease with which it fit into their home. Others were former Apple devotees, flocking back to the quirky company they once adored.

Fun Facts

Although Steve Jobs is not forthcoming about his personal life, an article on the Apple Museum website gives some fun facts about him. Here are a few.

His home: A red brick home built in the 1930s.

His heroes: David Packard, cofounder of Hewlett Packard; Bob Noyce, cofounder of Intel; and singer Bob Dylan.

His close friends: Former California governor Jerry Brown; Lawrence J. Ellison, billionaire businessman; and his sister Mona Simpson.

Favorite clothes: Jeans, black turtleneck shirts, and running shoes.

His car: A Mercedes-Benz.

Connections to famous people: He dated singer Joan Baez; he hosted former president Bill Clinton and Hillary Clinton at his home in Palo Alto and spent the night in the Lincoln Bedroom in the White House.

Most Prestigious Award: National Technology Medal with Steve Wozniak from President Reagan in 1985.

Information taken from http://theapplemuseum.com/index.php?id=49.

The bright colors on iMacs set Apple computers apart from other competitors.

Taking advantage of the machine's success, Jobs insisted Apple come out with a laptop version of the machine called the iBook a year later. It became the best selling laptop computer of its time. As a result, Apple's stock rose to record highs.

iTunes, iPod, and a Music Revolution

Jobs's next step was even more radical. Taking Apple's "Think Different" campaign to heart, he decided to take the company in a completely new direction. It would change the music industry forever.

Jobs always loved music. When he and Wozniak first met their love of Bob Dylan's and the Beatles' music helped bond them together. Jobs imagined consumers using their computers as a digital jukebox. There was already software available that could play digital sound files on a computer. But it was complicated to use. Jobs bought the rights to this software and had Apple engineers simplify it so that Apple owners could easily copy songs from compact discs (CDs) onto their computers. Jobs named this program iTunes.

Now that Apple users could store their favorite songs on their

Jobs introduces Apple's iTunes and iPod, allowing people to buy and manage their own music library.

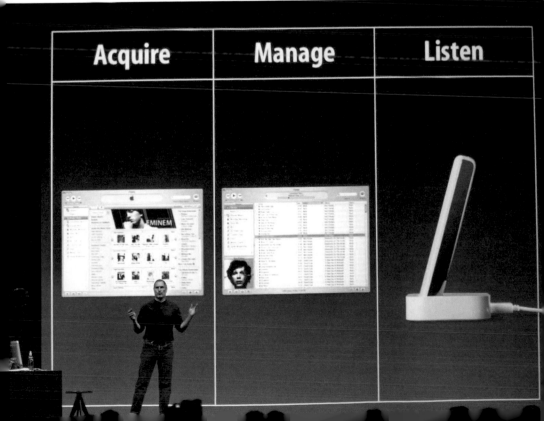

computer, Jobs turned his attention to coming up with a portable device that individuals could transfer their music onto and take with them everywhere. The device was named the iPod.

Similar devices known as MP3 players were already available, but they were clumsy, unattractive, difficult to use, and did not hold many songs. As a music lover, Jobs craved a better way to listen to music; so did many members of his Apple team. So Jobs decided to create it.

With that in mind, Jobs insisted that the iPod have excellent sound, be so simple to use that listeners could access any song they wanted in less than three pushes of a button, and be capable of holding one thousand songs. In addition, he insisted the device be small and stylish. While it was in development he constantly checked and rechecked the device for design, sound, and ease of use. He was not satisfied until it fit his specifications. "We did iTunes because we all love music. We made what we thought was the best jukebox in iTunes," he explains. "Then we all wanted to carry our whole music libraries around with us. The team worked really hard and the reason that they worked so hard is because we all wanted one. You know? The first few hundred customers were us."[55]

The iPod was released in October 2001. It turned out to be Apple's best selling product yet. It also changed the way people listened to music forever. But Jobs was not finished yet. At the time, many people were downloading music and trading music files via the Internet, without paying for them. Such action was not simple, was illegal, and hurt the music industry. Jobs got the idea of setting up an online music store, known as the iTunes Music Store, which would allow consumers to download their favorite songs for ninety-nine cents per tune. It would be inexpensive, legal, simple to do, and give music lovers access to thousands of songs, including new releases.

Jobs was sure that his idea was the way music would be distributed and sold in the future. He explains:

When we created the iTunes Music Store, we did that because we thought it would be great to be able to buy music electronically . . . I mean, it just seemed like the writing on the wall, that eventually all music would be distributed electronically. That seemed obvious because why have the cost? The music industry has huge returns. Why have all this overhead when you can just send electrons around easily?[56]

At first, the recording industry, which was used to distributing and selling music in the traditional way, did not agree with him. But Jobs never had a problem bending others to his will. His persuasiveness and clarity of vision convinced music industry executives and artists that it was a good idea. The iTunes Music Store opened in April 2003. In its first day, 275,000 songs were downloaded. A year later, more than 85 million songs had been

Apple Retail Stores

Apple retail stores are another of Jobs's successful creations. The stores sell everything Apple makes, giving consumers a convenient place to learn about and try Apple's products.

The first store opened in Virginia in 2001. As of 2009, there are 251 stores located throughout the world. The stores are all stylishly designed. Many have won architectural awards. All contain a Genius Bar, where customers can ask questions, get technical support, and have products repaired.

Newer stores have a studio where customers can get help in all sorts of creative ventures. The stores offer free group workshops and one-on-one personal training. There are also special programs for children, including Apple Summer Camp where kids can take free classes in digital photography, movie making, and other topics.

The stores are extremely popular. New store openings have become big events drawing crowds of people who often line up outside the store the night before. Usually the first one thousand customers are given free gifts such as commemorative tee shirts and goodie bags.

downloaded. By 2008 it had become the largest retailer of music in the United States. Moreover, it permanently changed the way music is sold and distributed. Once again Jobs's vision of the future seemed to be just what the public wanted.

Facing Death

It looked like Jobs's life could not get any better. He had a wonderful family who he adored. Pixar was doing well. And, he had turned things around at Apple. In 2000, he had finally agreed to become the CEO of Apple, accepting ten million shares of the company's stock, which was worth over $800 million.

Then in 2004, his seemingly perfect life came crashing down. Jobs was diagnosed with pancreatic cancer, a disease from which 90 percent of patients die within a year. At the time, the doctor told Jobs that the disease was incurable and usually carried a life expectancy of less than one year. But later in that day, the doctor performed a procedure, which involved retrieving a sample of cancer cells, in order to study the cancerous tumor more carefully. Jobs had an extremely rare slow-growing form of pancreatic cancer that, in some cases, surgery can cure. At first, Jobs resisted having surgery, believing he could cure the disease by eating a special diet. When that did not work, he had the surgery, which left him cancer free.

Jobs recalls what happened:

I had a scan at 7:30 in the morning, and it clearly showed a tumor on my pancreas. I didn't even know what a pancreas was. The doctors told me this was almost certainly a type of cancer that is incurable and that I should expect to live no longer than three to six months. My doctor advised me to go home and get my affairs in order, which is doctor's code for prepare to die. . . . I lived with that diagnosis all day. Later that evening, I had a biopsy, where they stuck an endoscope down my throat, through my stomach and into my intestines, put a needle into my pancreas and got a few cells from the tumor. . . . it turned out to be a rare form of pancreatic

> The reports of my death are greatly exaggerated.

In 2004 Jobs was diagnosed with pancreatic cancer and addressed his illness publicly.

cancer that is curable with surgery. I had the surgery and I'm fine now. This was the closest I've been to facing death and I hope it's the closest I get for a few more decades.[57]

Jobs's brush with death caused him to look at the direction his life was taking. It was not too late to make changes. But he found he did not need to. He was happy with his life. "One thing that came out most clearly from this whole experience," he explains. "I realized that I love my life. I really do. I've got the greatest family in the world and I've got my work. And that's pretty much all I do. I don't socialize much or go to conferences. I love my family, and I love running Apple and I love Pixar. And I get to do that. I'm very lucky."[58]

Moving Forward

Jobs did not let his coworkers know about his illness until after his surgery. A month later, he returned to Apple part-time. Soon, he was back full strength. Under his guidance, Apple continued creating more innovative devices that Jobs believed the public would love. One of the most inventive was the iPhone, which debuted in 2007. It was a stylish, simple to use cellular phone, which also served as a handheld mini-computer. With it, Jobs reinvented the telephone. It was the first device of its kind.

Jobs got the idea for the phone because he did not like his cell phone. He wanted a phone with more power and versatility. If, he reasoned, Apple could install the same operating system on a cell phone as they used on their computers, the phone would have much the same capabilities of a computer. And, since Apple had already worked with miniaturizing technology with the iPod, creating such a device did not seem like an impossible task. He explains:

> We all had cell phones. We just hated them, they were awful to use. The software was terrible. The hardware wasn't very good. We talked to our friends and they all hated their cell phones too. Everybody seemed to hate their phone. And we saw that these things really could become much more powerful and interesting to license. . . . It was a great challenge. Let's make a great phone that we fall in love with. And we've got the technology. We've got the miniaturization from the iPod. We've got the sophisticated operating system from Mac. Nobody had ever thought about putting an operating system as sophisticated as OS X inside a phone, so that was a real question. We had a big debate inside the company whether we could do that or not. And that was one where I had to adjudicate it and just say, "We're going to do it. Let's try." The smartest software guys were saying they can do it, so let's give them a shot. And they did.[59]

The iPhone was a huge success. And, although Jobs was deeply involved with Apple, he had not forgotten about Pixar. Under Jobs's leadership, the company was producing one blockbuster hit after another. By 2001, Pixar had earned $2.5 billion, making it one of the most successful movie studios of all time.

In 2003, Disney's contract with Pixar ran out. It took years for Jobs to negotiate another contract to his liking. He knew that

The iPhone was a cell phone and a mini-computer and became a phenomenon.

one of the reasons for Pixar's success was that he had given the company's creative division free reign to work their magic. Jobs refused to accept any deal that limited their creative freedom.

In 2006, Jobs and the Disney Corporation finally came to an agreement. Jobs sold stock shares of Pixar to Disney. However, the deal did not remove Jobs from Pixar. Instead, it made Jobs the largest shareholder in Disney. Jobs was now the chairman of Disney's board of directors. The deal also put John Lassiter, the head of Pixar's creative division, in charge of both Pixar's and Disney's animation studios, which guaranteed that Pixar's creative team would not lose the freedom to practice their art without interference.

Jobs thought that the deal was not only good for Pixar, but

also for Apple. Someday, he predicted, Apple technology would deliver Disney content. "We've been talking about a lot of things," he explains. "It's going to be a pretty exciting world looking ahead over the next five years."[60]

The Future

Jobs's ongoing vision of ever newer and better technology continues to make the world more exciting. However, there have been some recent bumps in the road. In early 2009, Jobs took a leave of absence from Apple due to health reasons. There was speculation that his cancer had returned, which Jobs denied. For undisclosed reasons, Jobs received a liver transplant in the spring of 2009. He returned to work on a part-time basis at the end of June.

Even if his health makes it impossible for him to work as long and hard as he has done in the past, the rebellious young man, who dreamed of bringing technology into everyone's life, has more than achieved his goal. He was not afraid to be different. In fact, he celebrated it. He built a whole company around it. Nor was he afraid to take risks.

No one knows what the future holds for Steve Jobs. But one thing is certain, he did what many thought was impossible. He changed the world.

Notes

Introduction: On His Own Terms

1. Quoted in Jeffrey S. Young, *Steve Jobs: The Journey is the Reward*. New York: Lynx Books, 1988, p. 42.
2. Jeffrey S. Young and William L. Simon, *iCon: Steve Jobs, the Greatest Second Act in the History of Business*. Hoboken, NJ: John Wiley, 2005, p. 33.
3. David A. Kaplan, *The Silicon Boys and Their Valley of Dreams*. New York: William Morrow, 1999, p. 99.
4. Steve Jobs (Commencement Address), "'You've Got to Find What You Love,' Jobs Says," *Stanford Report*, June 14, 2005. http://news-service.stanford.edu/news/2005/june15/jobs-061505.html?view=print.
5. Jobs, "'You've Got to Find What You Love,' Jobs Says."

Chapter 1: A Difficult Start

6. Robert X. Cringely, *Accidental Empires: How the Boys of Silicon Valley Make Their Millions, Battle Foreign Competition, and Still Can't Get a Date*. New York: Harper Collins, 1996, p. 197.
7. Quoted in Smithsonian Institution Oral and Video Histories, "Steve Jobs," April 20, 1995. http.//americanhistory.si.edu/collections/comphist/sj1.html.
8. Quoted in Smithsonian Institution Oral and Video Histories, "Steve Jobs."
9. Quoted in Young, *Steve Jobs: The Journey is the Reward*, p. 24.
10. Kaplan, *The Silicon Boys and Their Valley of Dreams*, p. 83.
11. Quoted in Smithsonian Institution Oral and Video Histories, "Steve Jobs."
12. Young and Simon, *iCon*, p. 12.
13. Quoted in Michael Moritz, *The Little Kingdom: The Private Story of Apple Computer*. New York: William Morrow, 1984, p. 39.

14. Quoted in Young, *Steve Jobs: The Journey is the Reward*, p. 28.
15. Steve Wozniak and Gina Smith, *iWoz: Computer Geek to Cult Icon: How I Invented the Personal Computer, Co-founded Apple, and Had Fun Doing It.* New York: W.W. Norton, 2006, p. 88.
16. Young and Simon, *iCon*, p. 16.
17. Quoted in Young and Simon, *iCon*, p. 17.
18. Kaplan, *The Silicon Boys and Their Valley of Dreams*, p. 85.

Chapter 2: Searching for Answers

19. Quoted in Kaplan, *The Silicon Boys and Their Valley of Dreams*, p. 85.
20. Quoted in Moritz, *The Little Kingdom*, p. 88.
21. Quoted in Moritz, *The Little Kingdom*, p. 89.
22. Quoted in Young, *Steve Jobs: The Journey is the Reward*, p. 59.
23. Quoted in Moritz, *The Little Kingdom*, p. 91.
24. Quoted in Young and Simon, *iCon*, p. 22.
25. Jobs, "'You've Got to Find What You Love,' Jobs Says."
26. Steve Wozniak, "Letters-General Questions Answered," *Woz.org*, March 1, 2000. http://www.woz.org/letters/general/91.html.
27. Quoted in Young and Simon, *iCon*, p. 23.
28. Quoted in Kaplan, *The Silicon Boys and Their Valley of Dreams*, p. 86.
29. Wozniak and Smith, *iWoz*, p. 147.
30. Quoted in Moritz, *The Little Kingdom*, p. 98.
31. Moritz, *The Little Kingdom*, p. 111.
32. Wozniak and Smith, *iWoz*, p. 157.
33. Wozniak and Smith, *iWoz*, p. 170.

Chapter 3: "We Will Have a Company"

34. Wozniak and Smith, *iWoz*, p. 172.
35. Quoted in Young, *Steve Jobs: The Journey is the Reward*, p. 97.
36. Quoted in Moritz, *The Little Kingdom*, p. 138.

37. Wozniak and Smith, *iWoz*, p. 212.
38. Quoted in George Gendron, "The Entrepreneur of the Decade: An Interview with Steve Jobs," *Inc.com*, April 1989. http://www.inc.com/magazine/19890401/5602.html.
39. Moritz, *The Little Kingdom*, p. 191.
40. Quoted in Betsy Morris, "Steve Jobs Speaks Out," *CNNMoney.com*, March 7, 2008. http://money.cnn.com/galleries/2008/fortune/0803/gallery.jobsqna.fortune/5.html.

Chapter 4: Down but Not Out

41. Quoted in Gary Wolf, "Steve Jobs: The NeXT Great Thing," *Wired*. http://www.wired.com/wired/archive/4.02/jobs_pr.html.
42. Quoted in Young and Simon, *iCon*, p. 62.
43. Leander Kahney, "We're All Mac Users Now," *Wired*, January 6, 2004. www.wired.com/print/gadgets/mac/news/2004/01/61730.
44. Quoted in Peter Elkind, "The Trouble with Steve," *Fortune*, March 17, 2008, p. 88.
45. Quoted in G.C. Lubenow and M. Rogers, "Jobs Talks about his Rise and Fall," *Newsweek*, December 30, 1995, p. 51.
46. Quoted in Alan Deutschman, *The Second Coming of Steve Jobs*. New York: Broadway Books, 2000, p. 46.
47. Young and Simon, *iCon*, p. 167.
48. Quoted in Young and Simon, *iCon*, p. 182.
49. Quoted in Young and Simon, *iCon*, p. 160.
50. Quoted in Deutschman, *The Second Coming of Steve Jobs*, p. 237.
51. Quoted in Deutschman, *The Second Coming of Steve Jobs*, p. 236.

Chapter 5: Into the Future

52. Quoted in PBS, "The Nerds" (The Television Program Transcripts: Part 1), *PBS.org*. www.pbs.org/nerds/part1.html.

53. Quoted in Deutschman, *The Second Coming of Steve Jobs*, p. 291.
54. Quoted in Peter Burrows, "The Seeds of Apple's Innovation," *Business Week*, October 12, 2004. http://www.businessweek .com/bwdaily/dnflash/oct2004/nf20041012_4018_db083 .htm.
55. Quoted in Betsy Morris, "What Makes Apple Golden," *CNNMoney.com*, March 3, 2008. http://money.cnn .com/2008/02/29/news/companies/amac_apple.fortune/ index.htm.
56. Quoted in Morris, "What Makes Apple Golden."
57. Jobs, "'You've Got to Find What You Love,' Jobs Says."
58. Quoted in Burrows, "The Seeds of Apple's Innovation."
59. Quoted in Morris, "What Makes Apple Golden."
60. Quoted in Peter Burrows and Ronald Grover, "Steve Jobs's Magic Kingdom," *Business Week*, February 6, 2006. http:// www.businessweek.com/magazine/content/06_06/b3970001 .htm.

1955

Steven Paul Jobs is born on February 24, 1955, in San Francisco, California.

1960

The Jobs family moves to the Silicon Valley.

1968

Jobs meets Steve Wozniak.

1971

Jobs and Wozniak make and sell illegal blue boxes.

1972

Jobs graduates high school and goes to Reed College.

1973

Jobs drops out of college.

1974

Jobs gets a job at Atari. He goes to India. He returns to Atari upon his return from India. He reconnects with Wozniak.

1976

Jobs founds the Apple Computer Company with Steve Wozniak.

1978

Jobs's daughter Lisa Brennan-Jobs is born.

1980

Apple Computer becomes a publicly traded company. Jobs becomes a millionaire.

1982

Jobs takes charge of Apple's Macintosh Division.

1984

The Macintosh debuts.

1985

Jobs loses control of Apple. He starts NeXT.

1986

Jobs buys Pixar.

1989

Jobs meets Laurene Powell.

1990

Jobs marries Laurene Powell. His son Reed is born.

1991

Jobs makes a deal with Disney, which provides Pixar with financing.

1995

Jobs's daughter Erin is born. Pixar becomes a publicly traded company, making Jobs a billionaire.

1996

Apple buys NeXT. Jobs returns to Apple.

1997

Jobs becomes Apple's Interim CEO.

1998

The iMac debuts. Jobs's daughter Eve is born.

2000

Jobs becomes the CEO of Apple.

2001

The iPod debuts.

2003

The iTunes Music Store opens.

2004

Jobs is diagnosed with pancreatic cancer. He undergoes surgery and is cancer-free.

2006

Jobs sells shares of Pixar to Disney. He becomes the chairman of Disney's board of directors.

2007

The iPhone debuts.

2009

Jobs takes a medical leave of absence from Apple early in the year; he returns to work on a part-time basis at the end of June.

For More Information

Books

Ann Brashares, *Steve Jobs {Thinks Different}*. Brookfield, CT: Millbrook Press, 2001. A young adult biography focusing on Jobs's contribution to technology.

Jim Corrigan, *Business Leaders: Steve Jobs*. Greensboro, NC: Morgan Reynolds, 2009. A young adult biography spotlighting Jobs's life as a businessman.

Anthony Imbimbo, *Steve Jobs: The Brilliant Mind Behind Apple*. Milwaukee: Gareth Stevens Publishing, 2009. A young adult biography giving particular attention to Jobs's work with Apple.

Jeffrey S. Young, *Steve Jobs: The Journey is the Reward*. New York: Lynx Books, 1988. A fascinating book written for adults about Jobs's early life.

Periodicals

Peter Elkind, "The Trouble with Steve," *Fortune*, March 17, 2008.

George Gendron, "Entrepreneur of the Decade: An Interview with Steve Jobs," *Inc*, April 1989.

G.C. Lubenow and M. Rogers, "Jobs Talks about his Rise and Fall," *Newsweek*, December 30, 1995.

DVDs

Turner Home Entertainment, *The Pirates of Silicon Valley*. DVD Release 2005. A dramatization depicting the beginnings of Apple and Microsoft.

Web Sites

Apple Museum (http://www.theapplemuseum.com/index.php?id=49) This web site offers a wealth of information about Apple, its history, products, and people.

Folklore (http://www.folklore.org/index.py) A web site dedicated to Apple computers. It offers lots of interesting first person accounts from various people involved with Apple.

Smithsonian Institute Oral and Video Histories, "Steve Jobs," (http://americanhistory.si.edu/collections/comphist/sj1.html) This site offers a lengthy interview with Jobs conducted in 1995.

Steve Jobs Info.com (http://www.stevejobs.info/) This unofficial Steve Jobs fan web site offers articles, news, quotes, videos, and links.

Woz.org (http://www.woz.org/) Steve Wozniak's personal web site where he talks about everything including his partnership with Jobs.

Picture Credits

About the Author

Barbara Sheen is the author of more than forty books for young people. She lives in New Mexico with her family. In her spare time, she likes to swim, walk, cook, and garden. When she first became a writer, there were no personal computers. In order to revise her work, she had to retype everything. Her first computer was an Apple II. It made writing books a lot easier. She has Steve Jobs and Steve Wozniak to thank for that.